GRAND CANYON
NATIONAL PARK

POCKET PORTFOLIO®
–Number Two–

GRAND CANYON

NATIONAL PARK

including
OCEANS of TIME
by
STEWART AITCHISON

SIERRA PRESS
Mariposa, CA

Ridges below Yavapai Point, early morning, South Rim.

We would like to thank Ellis Richard and L. Greer Price of Grand Canyon National Park as well as June Malpino and her staff at the Grand Canyon Association for their assistance in the creation of this book. We would also like to take this opportunity to thank the many photographers who made their imagery available to us during the editing of this title—Thank You!

ISBN O-939365-52-9

Copyright 1997 by:
Tellurian Press, Inc.
4988 Gold Leaf Drive
Mariposa, CA 95338

Printed in Singapore. First Edition: Spring 1997. Second printing, Summer 2001. Third printing, Spring 2003.

Front Cover: Winter sunrise seen from Maricopa Point, South Rim.
Frontispiece: Ridges backlit by early-morning light, South Rim.
Title Page: Ridges backlit by late-afternoon light, South Rim.
Back Cover: Prickly pear cactus detail.

Wotans Throne and setting moon, early morning from Cape Royal, North Rim.

In 1699, the Spaniard Juan Manje may have been the first to use the name Colorado to refer to the river, but many years would pass before the name took hold. Explorer John Wesley Powell is credited with promoting the name Grand Canyon, which he may have borrowed from General William J. Palmer's 1868 railroad survey map. Powell and his crew endowed the canyon with many romantic and descriptive names. Geologist Clarence Dutton had a fondness for architectural and oriental terms. The topographers Francois Matthes and Richard Evans carried on the heroic nomenclature by using mythical, classical, and religious names including those from Arthurian legends. Turn of the century travelogue writers, the National Park Service, and visitors have also added a wide variety of names to the Grand Canyon's features.

Matkatamiba Canyon, near river level.

Aspens, North Rim.

I WAKE GASPING FOR BREATH AND SUDDENLY REMEMBER WHERE I AM SLEEPING—
on a sandstone ledge jutting out over the thousand-foot-deep Inner Gorge of the Grand Canyon. I can hear the roar of the Colorado River far below, but it's too dark to see the tumultuous
flow in the black abyss. I was dreaming that I was drowning at the bottom of a shallow sea. Only a
bad dream, or was it? I close my eyes, but sleep eludes me. The ground seems harder and lumpier
now. Trace fossils—the trails, burrows, and imprints of extinct creatures—underlie my bed. Some
550 million years ago marine tubeworms burrowed where my pillow now rests. Under my back,
trilobites, one of the earliest of all animals to possess eyes, plowed through the soft sea floor ooze
forming long, curvaceous, double-lobed ridges. And perhaps a primitive jellyfish left the four-inch
round depression that cups my right hip. Fortunately, the Cambrian ocean has retreated and I'm not
under water but more than a half-mile above the present sea level.

Summer sunset, Mather Point, South Rim.

By the 1890s, Grand Canyon was recognized as one of America's most scenic wonders. President Benjamin Harrison proclaimed the area the Grand Canyon Forest Preserve in 1893, but miners, stockmen, and settlers were quick to voice their opposition. In 1903, President Theodore Roosevelt visited the Grand Canyon for the first time and stated, "In the Grand Canyon, Arizona has a natural wonder which, so far as I know, is in kind absolutely unparalleled throughout the rest of the world...in your own interest and in the interest of the country...keep this great wonder of nature as it is now...". And although Roosevelt established Grand Canyon National Monument by presidential proclamation, not until 1919 did Congress finally pass legislation to create Grand Canyon National Park.

Utah agave, South Rim.

My mind drifts on this long vanished sea back to the first time I witnessed this awesome place called the Grand Canyon. Like millions of other tourists, my family came to the South Rim to see for themselves what all the fuss was about. As we pulled into the Mather Point parking lot, the surface of the earth suddenly dropped away and a breath-taking, yet unreal, view lay at our feet. The earth's very skin had been torn asunder, raw and exposed. The abrupt escarpment and the overwhelming expanse silenced all idle chatter. We slowly walked to the edge, clutched the guard rail, and peered in. And when we spoke only reverent whispers came out.

A summer afternoon thunderstorm had just washed the rocks and saturated the soil. In the bottom of the great canyon, ancient, wrinkled walls of dark somber browns and glistening blacks buttressed younger brighter layers of stone. Pistachio green inclines met sage green flats. Rosy cliffs supported vermilion ledges and crimson slopes. Golden tan escarpments held up porcelain white palisades.

Harding Rapid and Colorado River, Marble Canyon.

The statistics—one-half to eighteen miles wide, a mile deep, 277 river miles long—hardly begin to convey the awesome spectacle that is the Grand Canyon. The canyon is the epitome of the geologic forces at work on the Colorado Plateau. A third of the Earth's geologic history is exposed in its walls and slopes that stair-step from boreal forests on the North Rim to Sonoran-like desert at its bottom. And while geologists have unraveled many of the intricacies of each individual layer of rock, the details of the formation of the great canyon are still shrouded in mystery. Likewise, biologists have recorded and studied the diversity of plants and animals within its walls but have barely begun to understand the interrelationships of the canyon's dynamic and complex ecosystems.

The Esplanade at sunset.

Hopi guides led Spanish conquistador Don García López de Cárdenas to the South Rim in 1540. The Cárdenas party, more interested in finding gold, was apparently unimpressed, calling the canyon an arroyo. Not until the mid-nineteenth century did systematic exploration of the Grand Canyon region begin. Lieutenant Joseph Christmas Ives was charged with finding a supply route to army troops in Utah. He explored the lower Colorado River by steamboat but wrecked before reaching Grand Canyon. He continued overland, descending Diamond Creek to the inner depths of the Grand Canyon; and although he felt the trip was the event of his life, his official report contained the notorious statement: "Ours has been the first, and will doubtless be the last, party of whites to visit this profitless locality."

The view from the Colorado River at Mile 134.5.

I was seized with the irresistible urge to go down inside this fantastic, mysterious place. I had to see close up those rocks, those soaring cliffs, the river that had carved this masterwork of nature. But my dad, wiser and more sensible than I, said, "Maybe some other time." He was certain that my fool notion would pass.

Two years later, we were on the South Kaibab Trail, a steep, knee-wrenching path leading a vertical mile down to the Colorado River and Phantom Ranch—the only tourist accommodation within the park that is below the rim. We were not prepared for the ordeal, to say the least—shod in old street shoes, packing only a half-gallon, saddle blanket-covered, canteen (just like the one John Wayne used in his Westerns), and carrying a frameless canvas rucksack about as comfortable as strapping on a fifty-pound bag of potatoes.

Colorado River in Marble Canyon near Nankoweap.

The mid-August desert sun was turning this shadeless trail into a shimmering, fiery hell-hole. Through sheer naïveté, we marched forth undaunted or I should say skidded downward, attempting to keep gravity from pitching us over a cliff.

Blistered and parched, muscle-sore, and covered in red dust, we finally made it to the ranch. A swim in the icy cold pool (which unfortunately no longer exists) revived our spirits if not our bodies. Before dawn the next morning, we started up the Bright Angel Trail, a longer but less steep route to the South Rim. Eleven excruciating hours of walking later, we were on top. My dad announced in a weary voice, "I'm not doing that ever again!" And he kept his word. I, on the other hand, was hooked. Other canyon trails beckoned and I have heeded their call.

Vishnu Temple and Freyda Castle from Cape Royal, North Rim.

The Grand Canyon's most famous explorer has to be the one-armed Civil War veteran Major John Wesley Powell. In 1869, the 35-year-old self-taught scientist and a motley crew of nine men boarded four wooden boats in Green River, Wyoming and floated down into the great unknown. Ninety-eight days, a thousand miles, and countless rapids later, minus two boats and four members, Powell and the remaining men emerged from the Grand Canyon. Powell went on to eventually persuade Congress to create the United States Geological Survey and the Bureau of Ethnology, both of which he would lead; and in 1888, he helped establish the National Geographic Society. Of the canyon, he would say, "You cannot see the Grand Canyon in one view... you have to toil from month to month through its labyrinths."

Hilltop Ruin (Anasazi), Unkar Delta area, eastern Grand Canyon.

Long before the coming of European-Americans, Paleo-Indians, hunters of the Ice Age megafauna, may have visited the canyon, but no definitive evidence has been discovered. By 2000 B.C., the Archaic Culture was caching figurines made of split willow twigs and occasionally painting enigmatic murals of ghost-like beings. From about A.D. 700 to 1200, new groups of hunters and gatherers, who also practiced agriculture, built tentative settlements in the canyon. These Anasazi and Cohonina cultures abandoned the area after a particularly severe drought in the twelfth century. A century and a half later, the Cerbats, possibly the ancestors of the present-day Havasupai and Hualapai, arrived from the west to eke out a living along the south side of the canyon as Paiutes immigrated to the north side.

Havasu Falls, Havasupai Indian Reservation.

SOME SIX YEARS AND A COLLEGE DEGREE IN ZOOLOGY LATER, I FOUND MYSELF hiking down the abandoned Nankoweap Trail in the remote northeastern part of the park. Mid-March promised an early spring. Most of the snow was already gone in the high country following several weeks of mild temperatures. Clad in shorts, T-shirt, and properly broken-in hiking boots, I set off with two other biologists and several geologists for a week of exploring and study. At the time (1970), a cabin stood near the trailhead on Saddle Mountain, and we cached warm clothes and extra drinking water there for our return.

"Duck-on-a-rock" and North Rim seen through morning fog, winter.

John Strong Newberry, the geologist on Ives' expedition, remarked, "Nowhere on the earth's surface...are the secrets of its structure revealed as here." Almost 2 billion years worth of earth history is exposed in the walls of the Grand Canyon. The dark, somber metamorphic schist, gneiss, and granite of the Inner Gorge and the rusty orange, beige, black, and purple hues of tilted sedimentary layers (the Grand Canyon Supergroup), as seen from Desert View, are both remnants of mountain ranges so ancient that the mind is dumbfounded. Above the tilted layers, some 4,000 vertical feet of horizontal beds of sandstone, limestone, and shale have been eroded into alternating cliffs and slopes due to differences in hardness. Each of these layers contains fossils that illustrate the evolutionary march of life through time.

Fossils in limestone, Shivwits Plateau.

Unkar Delta seen from near Desert View, South Rim.

Our party was by no means the first to descend into this part of the canyon. Toward the end of the last ice age, some 11,000 years ago, Paleo-Indian hunters may have ventured off the rim into the Nankoweap basin in search of remnant herds of mammoths, camels, Harrington goats, and giant bison. Over the millennia other hunters and gatherers would pass through the canyon, sometimes leaving behind tantalizing yet enigmatic figurines fashioned from split willow twigs and painted panels of ghost-like beings. Centuries later, the Anasazi (Ancestral Pueblo peoples) and others came to hunt deer and bighorn sheep and to gather pinyon pine nuts. They stayed to build small cliff houses and occasionally larger settlements near their tended fields of corn, beans, and squash. However, a severe drought in the twelfth century forced them out of the canyon region. About three hundred years later, yet another hunting-gathering culture arrived on the scene—the Kaibab Paiutes. A deadly clash between the Paiutes and a group of Apaches near the head of this canyon resulted in the name *Ninkuipi* (later corrupted to Nankoweap), "the place where people were killed."

Then, in 1882, John Wesley Powell, the one-armed Civil War veteran who had successfully completed the first exploration of the Colorado River through the Grand Canyon in 1869, and his crew "...gradually overcame the apparently insurmountable obstacles..." to provide horse access into Nankoweap Canyon. Powell, who was by this time the director of the United States Geological Survey, led the eminent paleontologist Charles Doolittle Walcott to the trailhead to study the rocks of eastern Grand Canyon. Walcott spent seventy-two days in the inner canyon.

Fluted limestone at Hermit Creek Rapids.

During that time, he and his assistants blazed a trail along a major fault that runs west of, and is partly responsible for, the row of isolated buttes—Nankoweap Mesa, Malgosa Crest, Kwagunt Butte, Awatubi Crest, Chuar Butte, and Temple Butte—that tower over the Colorado River. Walcott eventually reached the Unkar Creek area before retracing his steps back to the North Rim.

    Within a couple years, horse thieves connected the Nankoweap Trail with a prospector trail on the south side of the river to form a cross-canyon route. The rustlers stole horses in Utah and drove them to Arizona to be sold. Horses stolen in Arizona and New Mexico were then taken to Utah, hardly an easy way to make a living. Not only was the trail long, precarious, and arduous but swimming the turbulent Colorado River could be fatal.

Lava flows and Colorado River from Toroweap Overlook (looking downstream).

The angular relationship between the tilted Precambrian Grand Canyon Supergroup below and the horizontal Paleozoic sedimentary layers above was named the Great Unconformity by Powell. He recognized that this sharp contact represented an extremely long period of time, a half-billion years or more, during which erosion beveled the older surface to a flat plain before a sea transgressed and deposited the younger sand, mud, and lime. During the last five to thirty million years, the Colorado River system has been excavating the Grand Canyon. In western Grand Canyon, at least twelve lava dams have blocked the Colorado River. The greatest of these formed 1.2 million years ago and created a lake more than 2,000 feet deep. Each lake eventually filled, overflowed its dams, and eroded it away.

Pinyon pine with fresh snow, South Rim, winter.

I wonder: did the outlaws notice the sea shell fragments imbedded in the Kaibab Lime-stone? Did they puzzle over the reptile tracks petrified in the Coconino Sandstone? Did they see the fern frond and dragonfly wing impressions in the Hermit Shale? As their horses kicked up dust going over the pass between Nankoweap Butte and Nankoweap Mesa, did these trail-hardened men ponder the origin of the odd-shaped stromatolite (calcareous algae) fossils common in the boulders along the trail? Were they ever fooled by the gold-colored spheres of marcasite (a relative of iron pyrite) eroding out of the ancient rocks?

The horse thieves rode into history and their trail faded, but we were still able to follow it with careful study of an old map. Finally, we dragged our spent bodies the last few yards to Nankoweap Creek, released ourselves from the bonds of heavy packs, and flopped on the ground. As I lay on my back, I enjoyed the wisps of high clouds turning pink in the fading light.

Rainbow and clearing storm seen from Yaki Point, South Rim.

The Grand Canyon is a place of extremes: more than one hundred inches of snow buries the North Rim in winter while, near the river, prickly pear cactus and other desert plants wait for a meager summer thundershower. On average, for every thousand feet of elevation loss, the temperature increases about three to five degrees Fahrenheit and annual precipitation decreases four to five inches. Thus, on the rim, temperatures are often twenty-five or more degrees cooler than along the river; a heavy downpour in the forest may completely evaporate before reaching the river. Additionally, the aspect of slope, the orientation of a particular canyon, cold-air drainage, anabatic winds, the seasonal path of the sun, and other factors help create a range of microclimates within the canyon depths.

Cottontop cactus near Saddle Canyon.

Aspen leaves, North Rim.

I T WAS PROBABLY MIDNIGHT WHEN I FELT THE DROPS OF ICY WATER splashing on my face. I turned over, certain that it was just a passing cloud. Drip, drip, drip. Okay, I had better get up. Since the weatherman had predicted continuing balmy spring weather, we biologists had left behind our real tent and only brought a cheap plastic tube tent. We strung a cord between two cottonwood trees and threaded the flapping, orange cylinder on to it. We three stuffed ourselves into the two-person shelter. The geologists fended for themselves.

Mount Hayden and fog seen from Point Imperial, North Rim.

During 1889, biologist Clinton Hart Merriam hiked down the Old Hance Trail to the bottom of the Grand Canyon, climbed the lofty San Francisco Peaks, and explored the austere Painted Desert. From his studies, Merriam proposed that plants and animals were arranged in broad horizontal bands—life zones—across the southwestern landscape according to altitude and temperature. At the canyon, five life zones can be found. In the inner canyon, where the vegetation and animal life is similar to the desert of northwestern Mexico, is the Lower Sonoran Life Zone. Coming up in elevation, the pinyon pine–juniper woodlands are in the Upper Sonoran. Next are the magnificent ponderosa pine forests—the Transition Zone. On the higher North Rim are the fir forests of the Canadian Life Zone and spruce–alpine fir forests of the Hudsonian Life Zone.

Pinyon pine and Utah juniper growing in fractures in the Kaibab Limestone, North Rim.

The first night passed tolerably, except for the occasional elbow in the side, rasping bouts of heavy snoring, and, of course, the ceaseless crinkling of the plastic walls. In the morning our geologic companions hoofed it south along the Butte Fault to study the oldest rocks exposed in the Grand Canyon—the Precambrian layers.

Over the next several days, thick, flannel-grey clouds hid the canyon rim and leaked a cold drizzle onto our camp. Dedicated scientists, we continued to perform our duties: collecting small mammals—animals like deer mice and pocket mice—and stuffing their tiny bodies with cotton and wire so that they could become part of a Park Service research collection. We noted the comings and goings of pinyon jays, ravens, and other birds and pressed plants for the park herbarium.

What has made the Grand Canyon? Weathering, erosion, transport. The rocks are weathered by the chemical action of air and water and of lichens and bacteria. Plant roots slowly widen fractures. Water seeps into the cracks, expands as it freezes, and the rock is wedged apart. The soft crumbly material now offers little resistance to erosion. Wind blows the finer material away; rain carries rock fragments downhill; gravity helps. Eventually most of this rock debris reaches the Colorado River where it is transported downstream. The river and its tributaries are responsible for the deepening of the main and side canyons; however, the outward growth or widening of the canyons is primarily due to gravity through weathering. Mostly it's a very slow process, but nature has an astounding abundance of time.

Granite Rapid and Dana Butte seen from river level.

The silt-laden Colorado River following local flashfloods.

In 1963, Glen Canyon Dam was completed upstream of the Grand Canyon. The river that was once "...too thick to drink, to thin to plow..." began to pool behind the concrete monolith. The annual scouring of spring floods was curtailed; about 90 percent of the mud, silt, and sand—the river's erosive agents—began to settle in the dead waters of Lake Powell. Now mostly clear, cold water is released through the dam's generators. Plants—some native, some not—have invaded the river banks creating new riparian habitats that allow certain indigenous animals to flourish and changing the migratory behavior of others. An experimental flood-size release from the dam in March, 1996 created at least fifty-five new sandy beaches which are welcomed by river runners for camping; washed out some of the exotic plants; and formed backwaters that may help the endangered humpbacked chub spawn. Someday though, Lake Powell will be choked with sediment; the lake waters will overtop the dam and "weathering, erosion, and transport" will release the wild river.

Newly formed beach at Mile 118 following the flooding of March, 1996.

On our last day, we packed our soggy gear and began to wend our way up the trail as the rain turned into sleet. None of us had long pants or heavy jackets, but the exertion of the steep uphill climb kept us reasonably warm—for a while. Somewhere between the rocks of the Mississippian and Pennsylvanian geologic periods, the sleet became honest snow. The dim trail was quickly disappearing under the falling flakes. We were soaked through, and the temperature was dropping. Retreat was in order. Between sliding on the mud and trying to find the trail, progress was agonizingly slow, but as darkness engulfed the canyon we arrived back at the creek.

Dog-tired, we restrung the tube tent, crawled inside, and fell dead asleep. The next morning dawned bitterly cold but amazingly bright and perfectly clear. A blue-banner sky arched across the chasm. Time to face the snowy trail again, provided that we could follow it all the way to the rim.

Aspens and pines in snow, North Rim.

Water is the magic that allows life. Rain and snowmelt seeps into the ground and travels down until it encounters an impervious rock bank such as shale or claystone. Then the water moves along the top of this bedding plane until it meets a cliff face, then it issues forth as a spring. Before the end of the last ice age, wetter and cooler climatic conditions allowed many plants and animals to have a wider distribution across the canyon's walls. However, as the American Southwest has become more arid, moisture-loving plants have retreated to the few remaining riparian areas and to the springs and seeps tucked into canyon alcoves. These secret hanging gardens may harbor maidenhair fern, scarlet monkeyflower, the recently discovered endemic MacDougall's flaveria, and the endangered Kanab ambersnail.

Vaseys Paradise, river level.

Twining snapdragon and maidenhair fern in Fern Glen Canyon.

Just as we were about to leave, the unmistakeable whomp, whomp, whomp of a helicopter reverberated throughout the canyon. Abruptly the chopper was upon us. The pilot was picking up rock samples left behind by our geologist friends and would be back in a few minutes to pick us up, too. The trailhead was buried by snow and the approach road had become a muddy quagmire, so we would have to be airlifted to the South Rim. What an odd sensation to be stomping around in the Precambrian desert and minutes later landing in three feet of powder snow in the midst of the Ponderosa pine forest.

Toroweap Overlook at sunrise, looking upstream.

THE THOUGHT OF THAT SPRING BLIZZARD SENDS A CHILL DOWN MY SPINE, and I am brought back to the moment. I snuggle a little deeper into my sleeping bag and gaze up at the spectacle of stars. I see Orion's belt and the bright star we call Rigel. The Havasupai, who live in western Grand Canyon, see *amu'u'*—a flock of bighorn sheep being ambushed by *hatakwila* (wolfman). The same stars but different stories.

My own Grand Canyon story spans nearly forty years. During that time, my relationship with the canyon has matured. Those first trips were tests of endurance and route finding followed by expeditions of research and scientific discovery. But now I return to the canyon as an old friend, a refuge from the ever increasing chaos of modern life, a sanctuary for my soul. The trails still challenge, but the stone walls are no longer silent to me. They speak of oceans of time, the ever evolving rhythm of life, the majesty and mystery of nature. I will soon need to break camp and hike to the rim and the outside world. But I will return.

Being here is coming home.

Summer rainstorm, late afternoon, South Rim.

Theodore Roosevelt insisted, "Leave it (the Grand Canyon) as it is....The ages have been at work on it, and man can only mar it. What you can do is to keep it for your children, your children's children, and for all who come after you...". Little did he know that in less than one hundred years, annual visitation would soar to more than 5 million. Ironically, most of these visitors are concentrated in just a few places along the rim, on a handful of trails, and along the Colorado River. Most of the canyon is rarely visited. And perhaps that's the way it should be—to be left alone in its majestic loneliness. In the short, human perspective, we need to be good land stewards so that we don't "mar it." But on the geologic time scale, nature will continue to rule, evolution will proceed, the canyon will erode away, and humankind may become just another blip in the fossil record.

—Other titles in the POCKET PORTFOLIO® Series—
Number One–Arches and Canyonlands
Number Two–Grand Canyon
Number Three–Mount St. Helens

FOR MORE INFORMATION

NATIONAL PARKS ON THE INTERNET:
www.nps.gov
GRAND CANYON NATIONAL PARK:
PO Box 129
Grand Canyon, AZ 86023-0129
(520) 638-7888
www.thecanyon.com/nps
Grand Canyon Association
PO Box 399
Grand Canyon, AZ 86023
(520) 638-2481
www.grandcanyon.org
CAMPGROUND RESERVATIONS (In the Park):
Biospherics
3 Commerce Drive
P.O. Box 1600
Cumberland, MD 21501
(800) 365-2267
HOTEL/MOTEL RESERVATIONS (in the Park):
Amfac Parks & Resorts
14001 East Iliff, Suite 600
Aurora, CO 80014
(303) 297-2757
www.amfac.com
REGIONAL INFORMATION:
The Grand Canyon Trust
2601 N. Fort Valley Road
Flagstaff, AZ 86001
(520) 774-7488
(520) 774-757- (FAX)
www.grandcanyontrust.org

CREDITS

Book Design: Jeff Nicholas
Text Editor: Nicky Leach
Photo captions: Stewart Aitchison
Photo Editor: Jeff Nicholas
Printing coordination: TWP, Ltd., Berkeley, CA
Printed in Singapore.

SUGGESTED READING

Aitchison, Stewart. *A WILDERNESS CALLED GRAND CANYON.* Stillwater, MN: Voyageur Press, Inc. 1991.
Carothers, Steven W. and Brown, Bryan T. *THE COLORADO RIVER THROUGH GRAND CANYON.* Tucson, AZ: University of Arizona Press. 1991.
Collier, Michael. *AN INTRODUCTION TO GRAND CANYON GEOLOGY.* Grand Canyon, AZ: Grand Canyon Association. 1980.
Hughes, J. Donald. *IN THE HOUSE OF STONE AND LIGHT: A HUMAN HISTORY OF THE GRAND CANYON.* Grand Canyon, AZ: Grand Canyon Association. 1978.
Leach, Nicky. *THE GUIDE TO THE NATIONAL PARKS OF THE SOUTH-WEST.* Tucson, AZ: Southwest Parks & Monuments Association. 1992.
O'Hara, Pat and McNulty, Tim. *GRAND CANYON NATIONAL PARK: WINDOW ON THE RIVER OF TIME.* San Rafael, CA: Woodlands Press. 1986.
Schmidt, Jeremy. *GRAND CANYON: A NATURAL HISTORY GUIDE.* New York, NY: Houghton Mifflin Co. 1993.
Schwartz, Douglas W. *ON THE EDGE OF SPLENDOR: EXPLORING GRAND CANYON'S HUMAN PAST.* Santa Fe, NM: The School of American Research. n.d.
Wilson, Jim and Wilson, Lynn. *GRAND CANYON: A VISUAL STUDY.* Mariposa, CA: Sierra Press. 1991.

PHOTO CREDITS

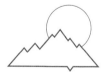

If you would like to receive a complimentary catalog
of our publications, please call:
(800) 745-2631,
or write:
SIERRA PRESS
4988 Gold Leaf Drive, Mariposa, CA 95338